ILLUSTRATION VOLUME TWO GUIDE

FOR ARCHITECTS, DESIGNERS AND STUDENTS

ILLUSTRATION VOLUME TWO GUIDE

FOR ARCHITECTS, DESIGNERS AND STUDENTS

BY
LARRY EVANS

WITH DRAWINGS BY
NANCIE WEST SWANBERG
AND DAN SMITH

 VAN NOSTRAND REINHOLD COMPANY
New York

26.96

4-23-90

I would like to thank Nancie West Swanberg for her tireless devotion to this book. She spent untold hours on this project and made a major contribution towards making this book a reality.

Advertisers, graphic designers, and craftspeople can make use of the illustrations in this book without securing permission. The only restriction is that you cannot reproduce the book as a whole or in substantial part.

Copyright © 1988 by Van Nostrand Reinhold Company Inc.
Library of Congress Catalog Card Number 81–71824
ISBN 0–442–22291–2 (volume 2)

Printed in the United States of America

Van Nostrand Reinhold Company Inc.
115 Fifth Avenue
New York, New York 10003

Van Nostrand Reinhold Company Limited
Molly Millars Lane
Wokingham, Berkshire RG11 2PY, England

Van Nostrand Reinhold
480 La Trobe Street
Melbourne, Victoria 3000, Australia

Macmillan of Canada
Division of Canada Publishing Corporation
164 Commander Boulevard
Agincourt, Ontario M1S 3C7, Canada

16 15 14 13 12 11 10 9 8 7 6 5 4 3 2 1

Library of Congress Cataloging-in-Publication Data

Evans, Larry, 1939–
    Illustration guide for architects, designers, and students.

    1. Architectural rendering—Technique.
2. Architectural rendering—Handbooks, manuals, etc.
I. Title.
NA2780.E9   1982   720′.28′4   81–71824
ISBN 0–442–22199–1 (pbk. : v. 1)
ISBN 0–442–22291–2 (pbk. : v. 2)

CONTENTS

The Hotel Netherland - New York City, circa 1890

INTRODUCTION

With the acceptance of <u>Illustration Guides For Architects, Designers and Students</u> as a valuable reference book, I undertook the task of providing a companion volume that would *work* with volume one rather than compete with it. The design of buildings and the nature of architectural illustration has changed considerably during my 30 years as an architectural delineator. Architects and designers now prepare many of their own illustrations instead of using professional delineators. Architectural illustrations are less formal than they were 30 years ago. Clients and planners seem to be more actively involved in the design process and more open to viewing design sketches.It is therefore even more important that the illustrator/designer have easy access to the entourage that will make the rendering more visually attractive.

Volume one delt more specifically with trees and how-to information. Volume two is slanted more towards figures. Using both volumes, the illustrator will find a vast range of material drawn in a variety of styles. Drawings are shown in several techniques from freehand sketches to formal technical illustrations. The figures are presented in several scales and even in no scale to allow for the right pose for your illustration - at the right size and facing in the right direction.

Architectural rendering is a valuable tool in the practice of architecture. A rendering can sell a design to a client as well or better than any other presentation. An architectural illustration may also be used to solicit tenants for space in commercial buildings. So it is imperative that your illustration be the very best that it can be.

It is my firm desire that the material presented in both volume one and this volume will be helpful to the illustrator by creating a handy file of drawings designed to add the finishing touch to any architectural illustration.

HOW TO USE THIS BOOK

Two main elements are required for creating a good rendering: perspective and composition. Composition is relatively easy as the center of interest is always the building (or a part of it). The very first thing you must do to begin your illustration is a "thumbnail" sketch. In this rough drawing you will attempt to solve several basic questions: 1) The size of the building in relation to the drawing paper, 2) The horizon line [eye level], 3) The vanishing points [the "view"] 4) The scale [especially for vertical height], 5) The placement of entourage (trees, autos, other buildings, etc.).

The "thumbnail sketch. If done accurately, this sketch will solve many problems in the final rendering.

SETTING UP A PERSPECTIVE

If you have plans and elevations to work from, then all the information regarding the building to be illustrated will be on them (except shadows). As the plans are done in scale, the placement of elements shown on the elevations within your drawing (also drawn to scale) should be easy. We'll assume for now that you are working on a sheet of tracing paper. You'll be using a 4H lead to establish the skeleton of your rendering and will switch to a 2H or softer lead to illustrate the entourage.

LAYING OUT THE BASIC ELEMENTS

Once you have taped your drawing paper into position, use your T-Square to draw a horizontal line. This line is the horizon line (also known as the eye-level line). Using the "thumbnail" sketch as a guide, you can establish where on the paper the horizon line should actually fall. Remember to save room for the sky. The next step is the creation of a measuring cube. This step will locate the "vanishing points" and establish the scale of the drawing. At this point you have several options concerning the view and how the building will appear.

ADJUSTING THE PERSPECTIVE TO SUIT YOUR NEEDS

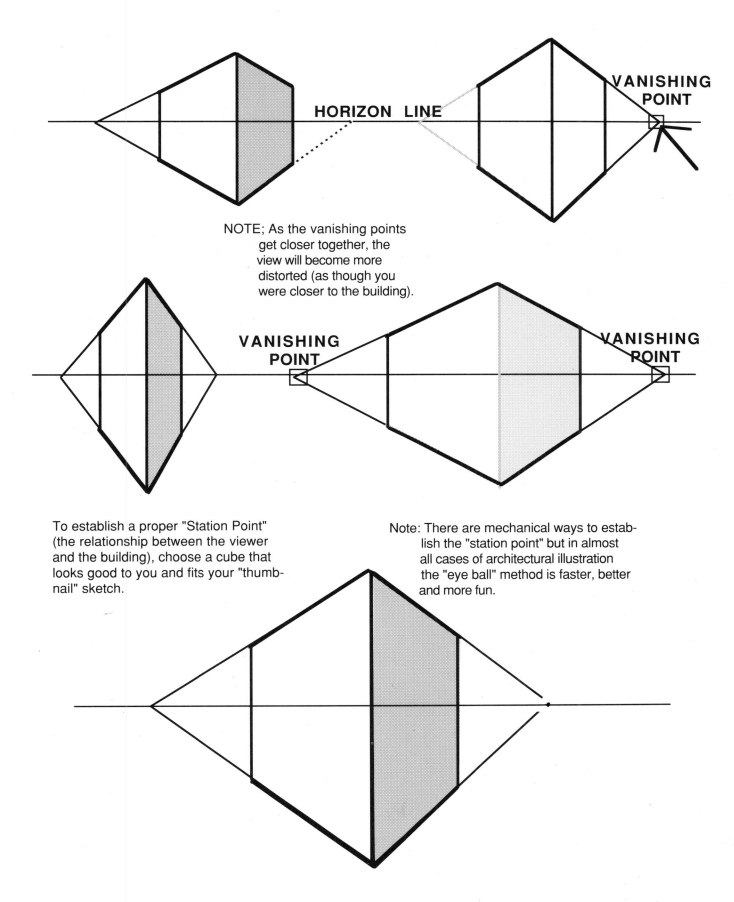

HORIZON LINE

VANISHING POINT

NOTE; As the vanishing points get closer together, the view will become more distorted (as though you were closer to the building).

VANISHING POINT

VANISHING POINT

To establish a proper "Station Point" (the relationship between the viewer and the building), choose a cube that looks good to you and fits your "thumbnail" sketch.

Note: There are mechanical ways to establish the "station point" but in almost all cases of architectural illustration the "eye ball" method is faster, better and more fun.

FITTING THE MATERIAL IN THIS BOOK INTO YOUR RENDERING

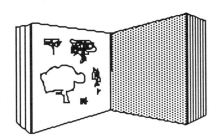

Trees, people, plants and vehicles are all shown in a variety of sizes. Look for the size closest to your needs and trace the image onto a thin piece of tracing paper.

When you have traced as much detail as you require, remove the tracing paper and using a soft (B or BB) pencil, lightly rub graphite on the back of the paper, completely covering the image.

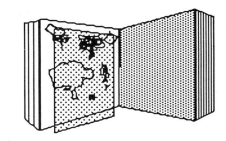

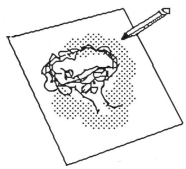

Rub the graphite with a tissue so the excess won't come off on your illustration paper. Of course if you're doing your sketch ON tracing paper, ignore all this.

Many copy machines can now make images to any size. You may find that you can create the image size you need by using such a machine. You can save time when doing your preliminary work by first copying the material to size and then pasting it onto your sketch. Then do the final tracing.

Note: It will save you time if you solve all of your layout problems BEFORE you start your finished drawing.

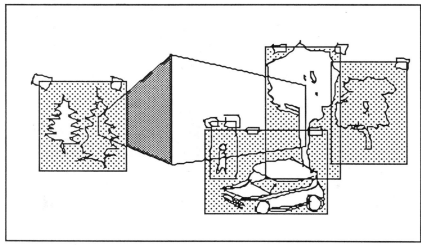

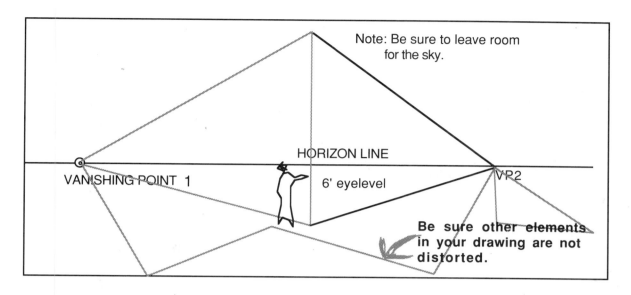

Note: Be sure to leave room for the sky.

HORIZON LINE

VANISHING POINT 1

6' eyelevel

VP2

Be sure other elements in your drawing are not distorted.

If your thumbnail sketch is a good guide, then the set-up of the perspective will go smoothly. You are now ready to develop the "measuring cube" so that you can locate windows, openings,etc. By using one of the scale figures in this book, establish an eye-level (6' for this demonstration). All the vertical measurements will now fall in scale on the "vertical height line". The creation of measuring points in perspective is a little more complicated but byusing the cube measuring system most dimensioning is simplified.

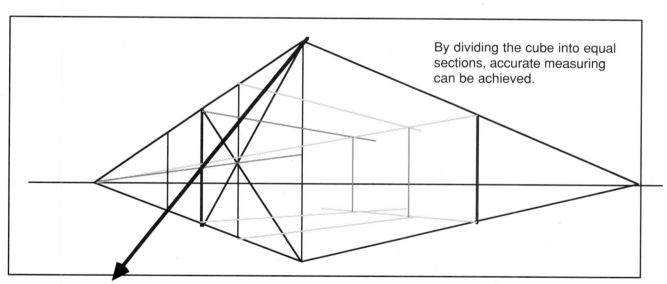

By dividing the cube into equal sections, accurate measuring can be achieved.

To project the cube forward or backward, just divide and build as you would any rectangle.

EARLY MASTERS OF RENDERING

EARLY MASTERS

This chapter contains a variety of some of the best illustrations created by past masters of renderings. Of these artists Joseph Pennell was possibly the best and certainly the most prolific.

Joseph Pennell (1860 - 1926) was a magazine illustrator who captured the essence of existing buildings. His ink technique is an excellent example of economy of line. His figures are superb and add a richness of scale and mood to his renderings.

Harry Fenn (1838 -1911) was a prolific artist who specialized in land-scapes and building illustration. He worked mostly in pen and ink but he was also a founder of the American Watercolor Society.

The way to apply these renderings to your illustration is to study the
line work and composition. Certainly trees and plants are the same today.
People are different enough so that modern poses must be used, but
the basic drawing is the same. Now that architectural design is swinging
back towards ornamentalism, reviewing some of the "old masters" sketches
can be usefuf for today's buildings.

Vestibule of the New York Life building, Minneapolis.

Harry Fenn did the illustrations on these two pages, probably about the size shown here. The perspective in the stairway above is wonderfully constructed using a unique station point just above the level of the landing. The drawing on the opposite page makes use of the foreground trees blending into the fabric of the structure but not obscuring it.

Madison Square Garden.

AT VIRE
FRANCE

The use of value patterns in the two illustrations shown here illustrate the basic requirement of preplanning your sketch. The tower above stands dark against a light sky with the toned foreground setting off the light middleground. The skyscraper grouping on page 7 sets off the light foreground building against its darker neighbor to the rear. No attempt has been made to deal with a near foreground as it would obscure the buildings on view.

New York skyscrapers circa 1900.

7

PROPOSED BUILDING AT SAN FRANCISCO.
WILLIS POLK, ARCHITECT.

THE CHATEAU · MARTAINVILLE
WEST FRONT

The material on the next four pages is taken from a German garden book printed around the turn of the century. The illustration technique is fresh and loose and allows for a good contrast between the foliage and the architecture.

Fig. 1.

Fig. 2

Fig. 3.

Fig. 4.

Fig. 12.

Fig. 13.

Fig. 14.

Fig. 15.

14

ACCESSORIES

Fig. 5.

Fig. 6.

Fig. 10.

Fig. 7.

Fig. 8.

Fig. 9.

Fig. 11.

Fig. 16.

Fig. 17.

Fig. 18

Fig. 19

Fig. 20.

Fig. 21.

Fig. 22.

Fig. 23

Fig. 24.

A turn of the century guide to architectural illustration.

CHATEAV · ST · AGIL
· FRANCE ·

16

RENDERING GALLERY

Ghirardelli Square - San Francisco

20

RENDERING GALLERY

The illustrations in this chapter were done by and large by the author. In some instances inking was done by Kahn Kay or Nancie West Swanberg. The reason for including these renderings in the book is to illustrate how the figures, trees and vehicles that make up the bulk of the text can be used in your drawings.
All the figures in the illustration of San Francisco's famed Ghirardelli Square (opposite page) are copied directly from this book. The trees and plants were drawn to fit the illustration but they were patterned after illustrations found in the tree and plant chapters.
Credit is given to the architects of the project when possible, but often the illustrations were done for owners, developers or just for advertising purposes and no architect was involved.

When inking, a pencil sketch is ALWAYS done first. Notice that the inked drawing below has changed somewhat from the pencil. It is almost impossible to make major changes in the ink drawing unless it is done on drafting film. If you ink on film, then the problem becomes how to color the image.

Architect - Sid Hoover/Robinson, Mills & Williams

The illustration above was done using the preliminary sketch shown on pages 26 and 27 The sketch on those pages is reproduced at full size. Most illustrations are reproduced at a much smaller size than the original drawing. In order for all the lines to hold, the illustrator must choose his or her pen sizes very carefully. This drawing was done using a #2 rapidograph for the street and foilage, a #0 for the buildings and a #00 for the people. A #000 nib was used for the brick indication.

The final ink drawing of this project is shown on page 25. This copy of the pencil layout is shown actual size. The figures were drawn in pencil on another sheet and inked first because they are in the foreground.

Architect - Robinson, Mills and Williams

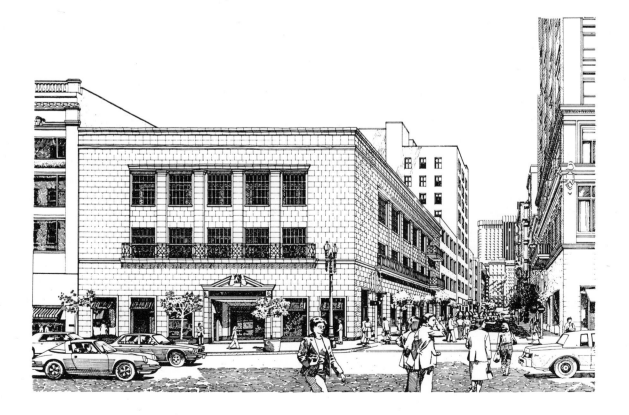

The renovation of existing buildings creates a special problem for the illustrator; the integration of existing elements as they relate to the new project. All the renderings on these two pages were done by using photographs, altered to fit each illustration's special requirement. For example: The bridge in the top drawing on page 28 was compiled from 3 photos taken from 3 different station points. The bottom illustration on the same page was made up of several photographs to widen the street and bring the background forward.

The trees in this rendering were drawn carefully in pencil before the final inking. They set the mood of the building even though the foreground is really just a parking lot.

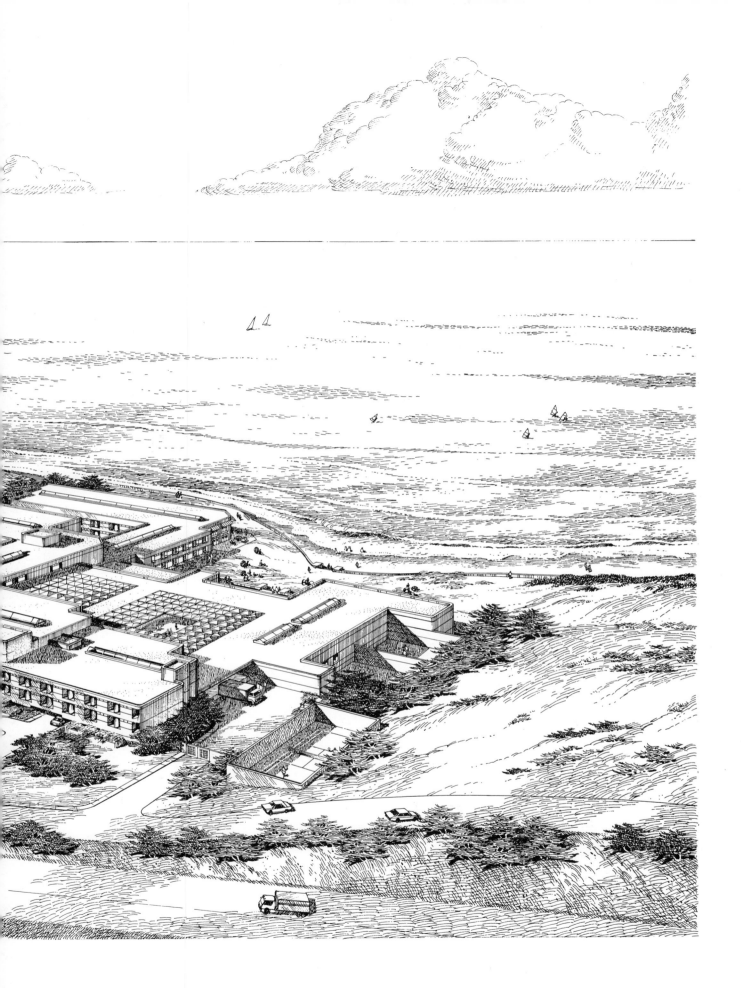

A proposed beachfront hotel. Notice how the trees have their trunks tucked in a bit to help the illusion of a high viewing angle.

The illustration above shows the pen and ink sketch from pages 32 and 33 after it has been colored. You can get more for your money by photographing your ink drawing in line before coloring, thus giving you two pictures for the price of one. I like to do my ink renderings on illustration board that has a couple of coats of gesso over the pencil drawing. You can still see the pencil but it won't photograph in line. When coloring the finished ink drawing, I use colored inks and watercolors to allow the ink lines to still show.

The illustrations on this page are of the same building. The watercolor sketch above was done during the early design phase and the ink and airbrush painting below was done after the working drawings were finished.

Architect - Lomax/Rock Architects/ Johannes Van Tilberg & Partners

SPARING OUT

The foreground trees in this drawing stand out from the background and add depth and interest to the picture. Plan your *sparing out* with a quick pencil sketch before the final inking.

The illustration of the shopping center uses a foreground building to offset the horizontal spread of the main building complex. The figures, trees and plants used in this rendering may be found in this book and in volume one.

Architect - Robinson, Mills and Williams

Architect - Robinson, Mills and Williams

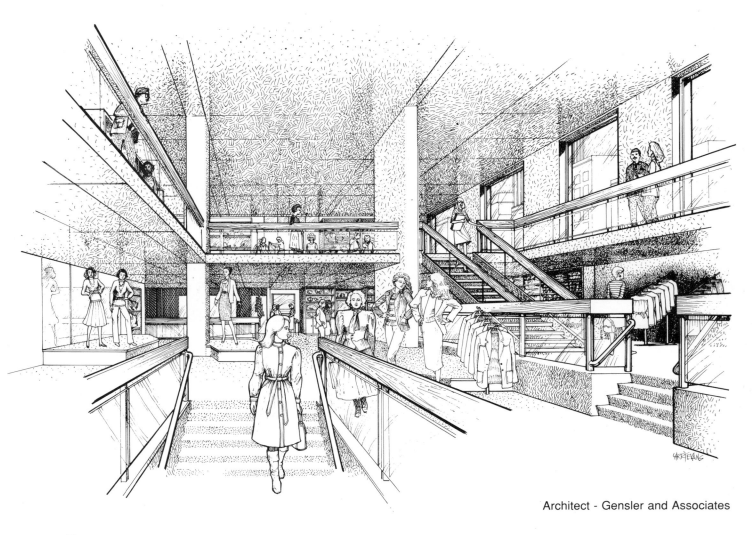

Architect - Gensler and Associates

40

Different inking techniques were used on all of these renderings.

The eye level of this rendering is about 3'. The design of the lobby didn't allow for a very high ceiling so the view had to be adjusted to compensate. Also, the lower eye level better illustrates the ceiling and its fixtures.

PEOPLE

FEMALE

SCALE 1/8" = 1'

SCALE 1/4" = 1'

46

60

SCALE 1" = 1'

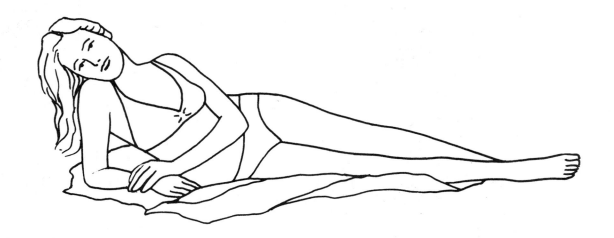

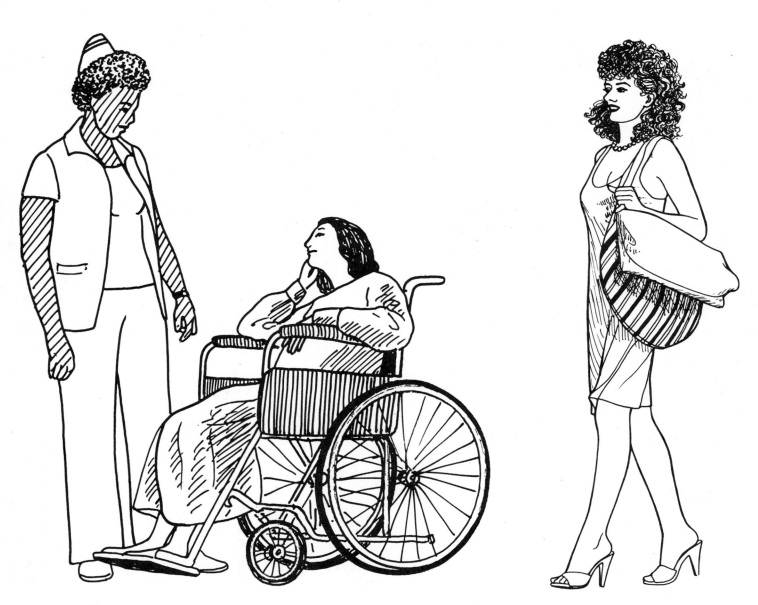

PEOPLE

MALE

When you draw figures at small scales (1/8", 1/4", etc.) consider what will happen
to the drawing when it is reduced. Be sure to simplify the figures enough so that the
lines will hold in reduction. Also, it is very difficult to try to copy the figures at a small
scale and show all the detail.

95

105

107

SCALE 3/4" = 1'

111

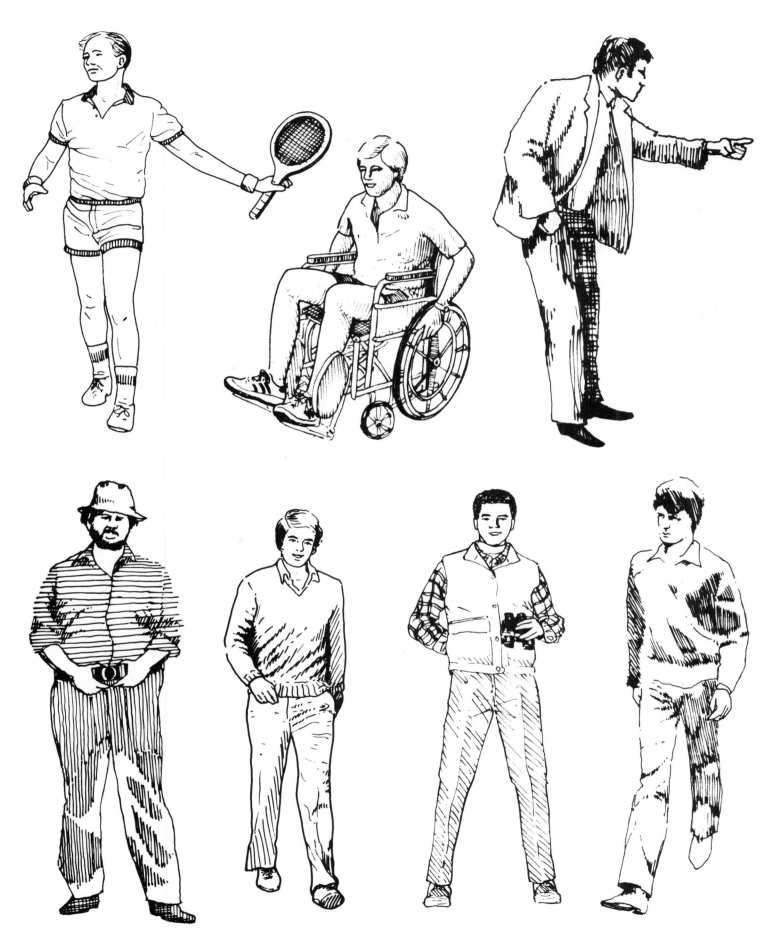

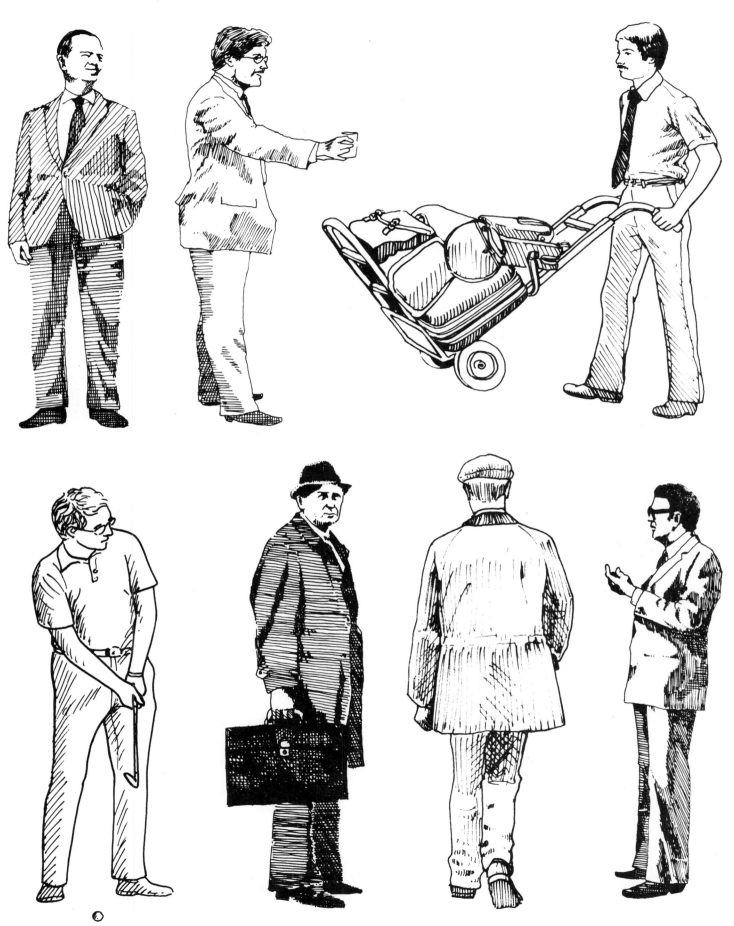

120

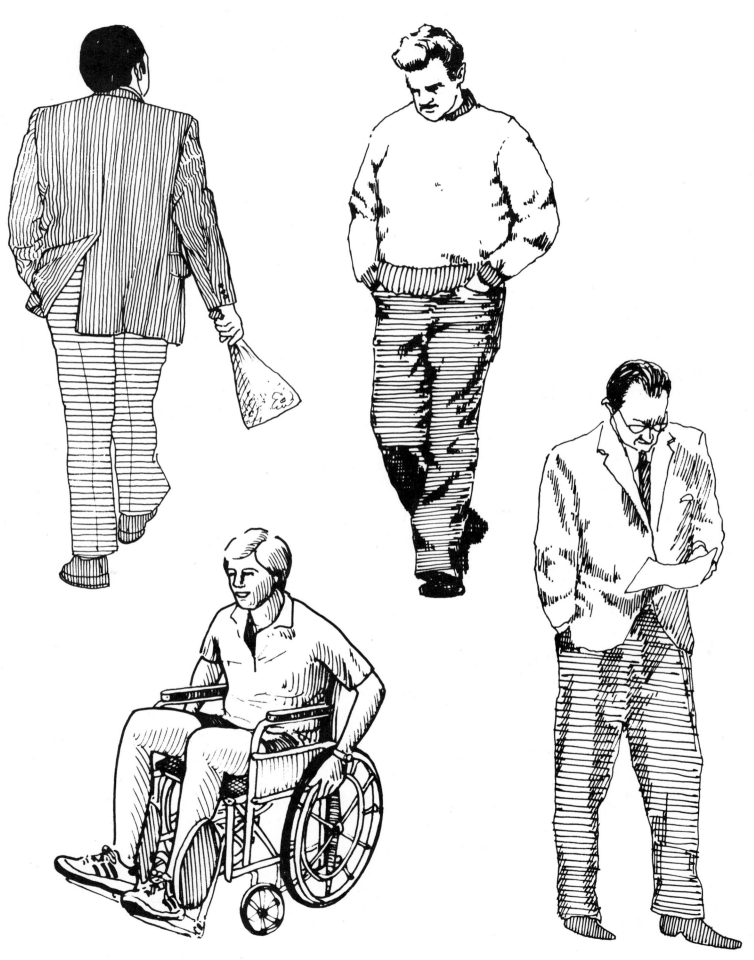

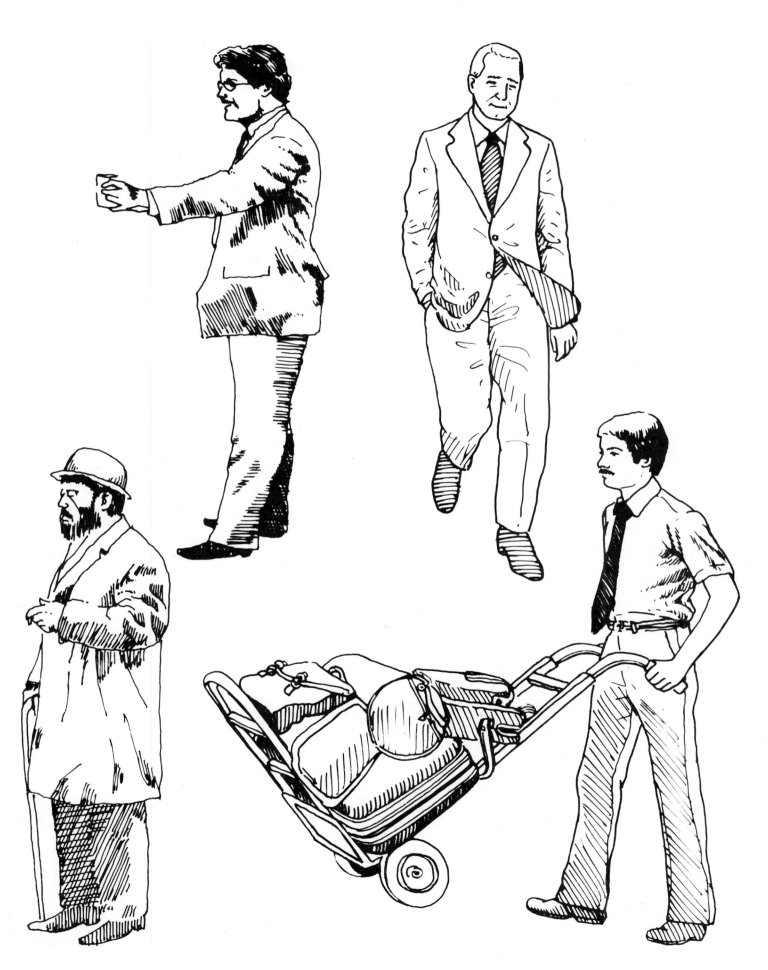

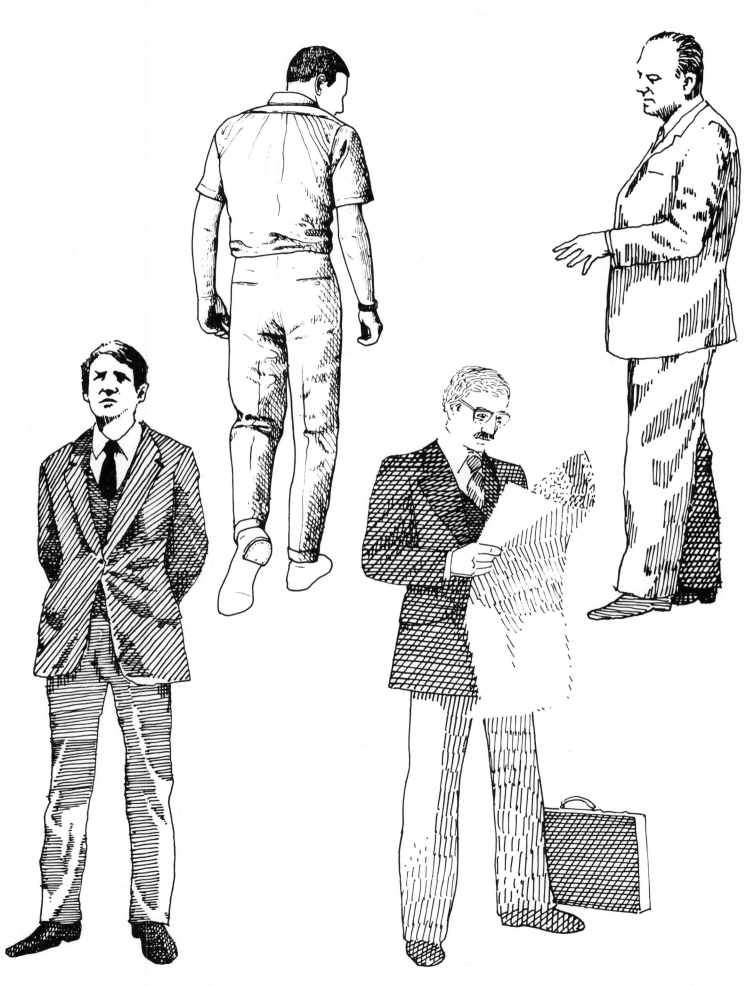

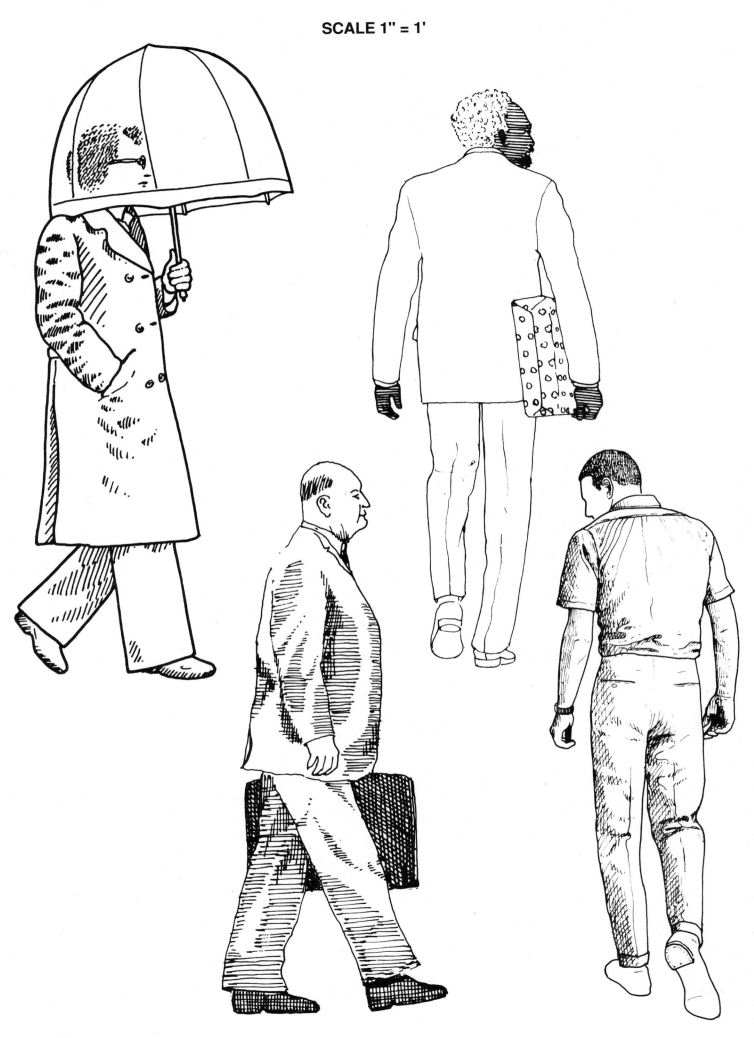

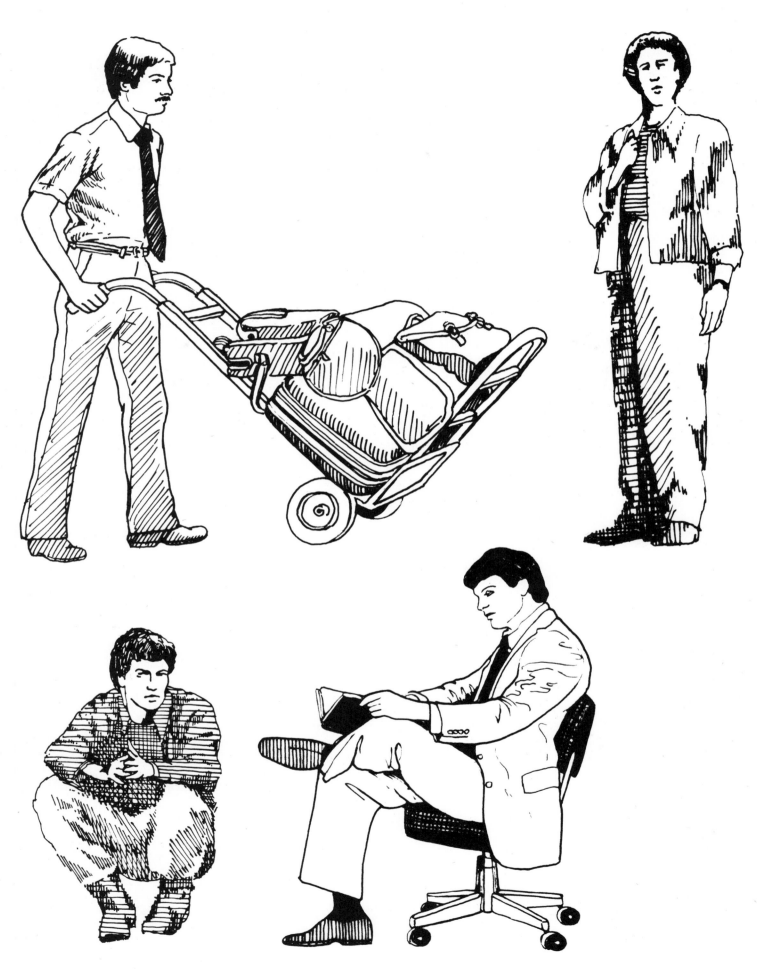

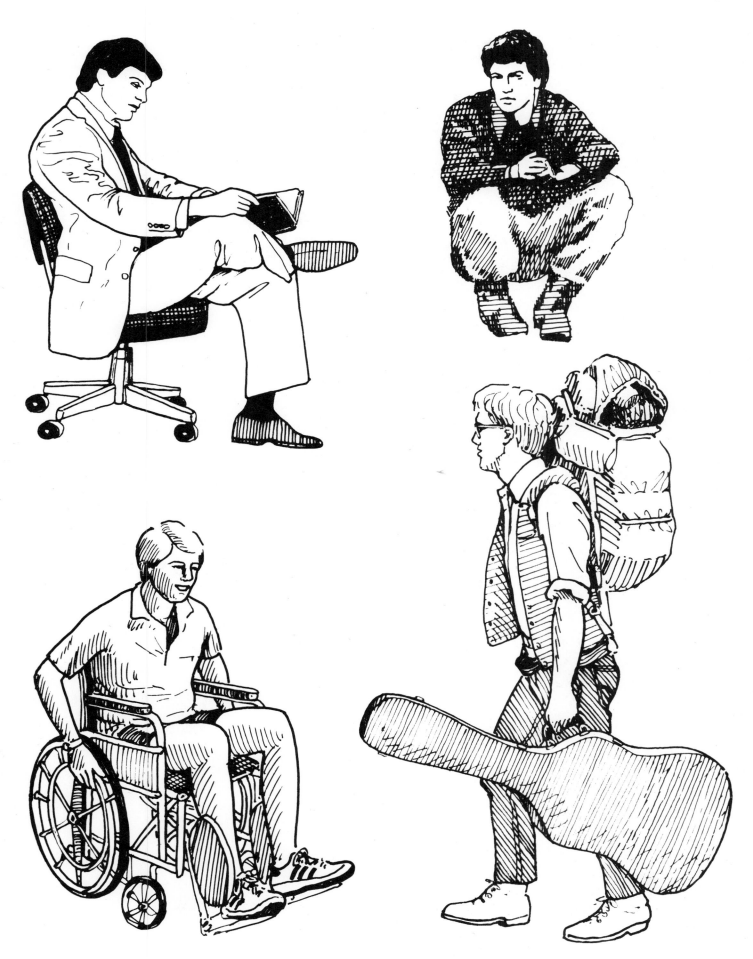

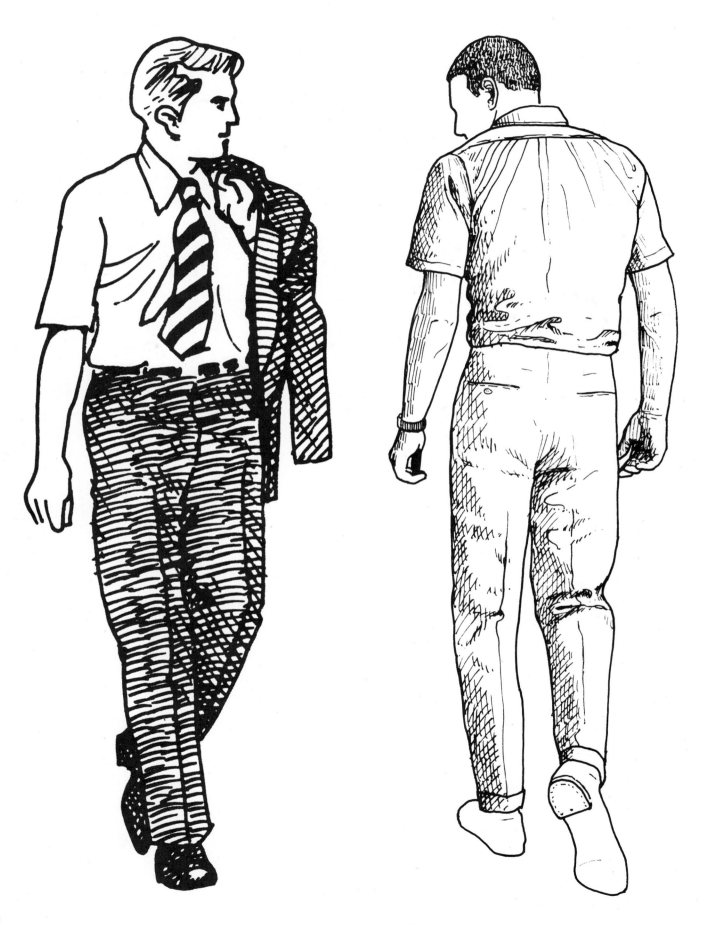

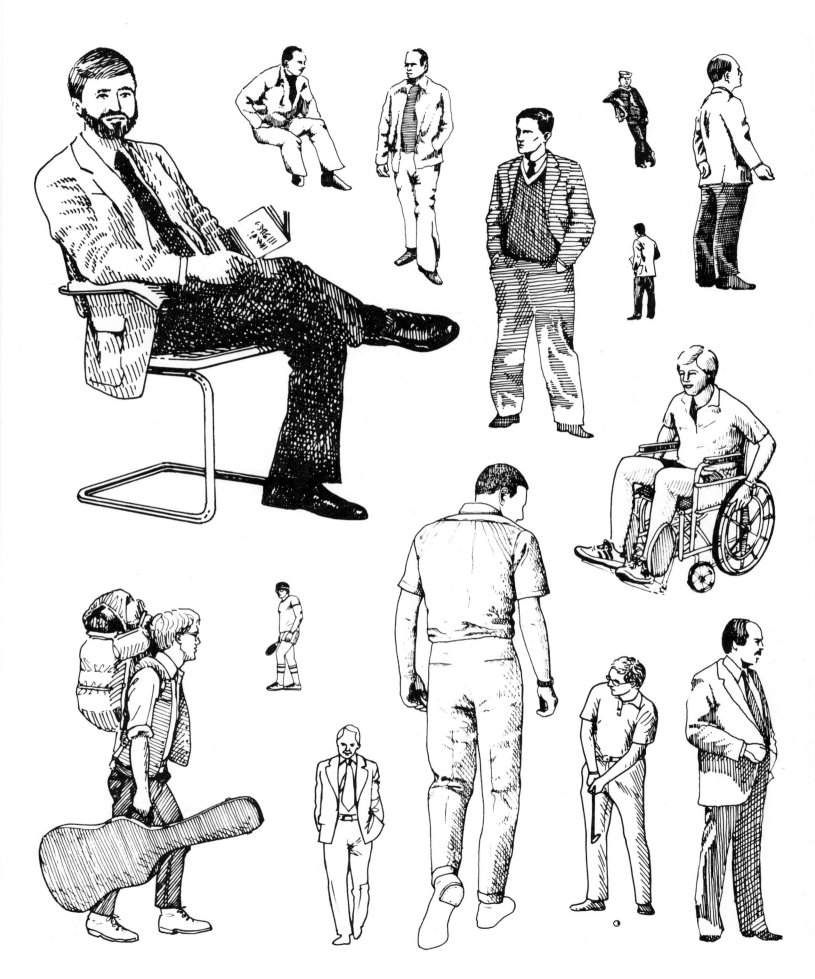

PEOPLE

GROUPS

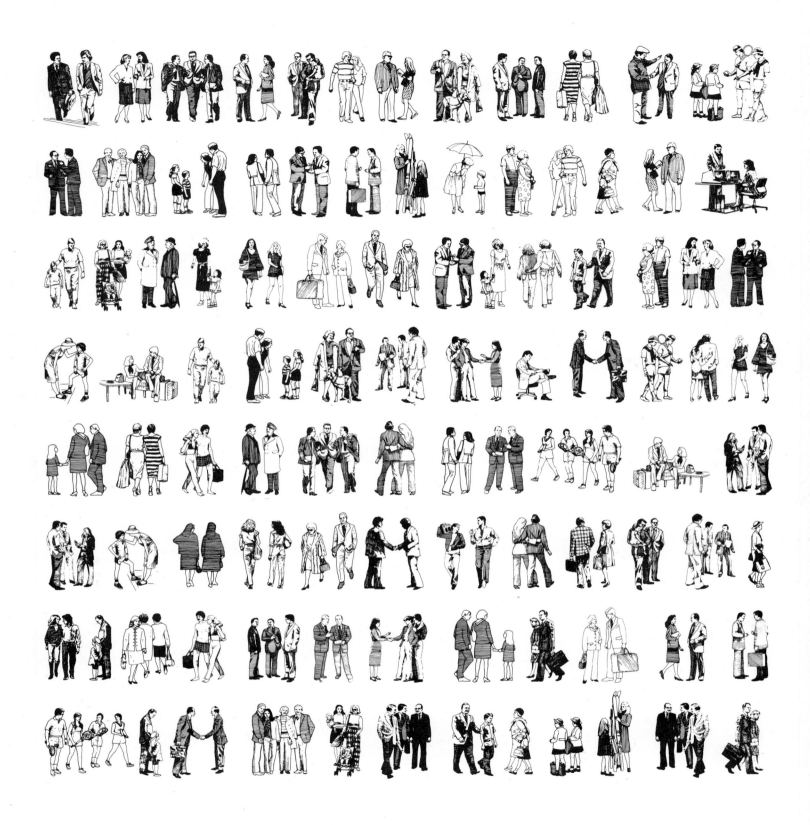

The figures illustrated in "groups" can be broken up and used individually. Some interesting combinations can be created, especially with the "children" section.

149

160

162

163

166

PEOPLE

CHILDREN

SCALE 1/8" = 1'

SCALE 1/4" = 1'

213

216

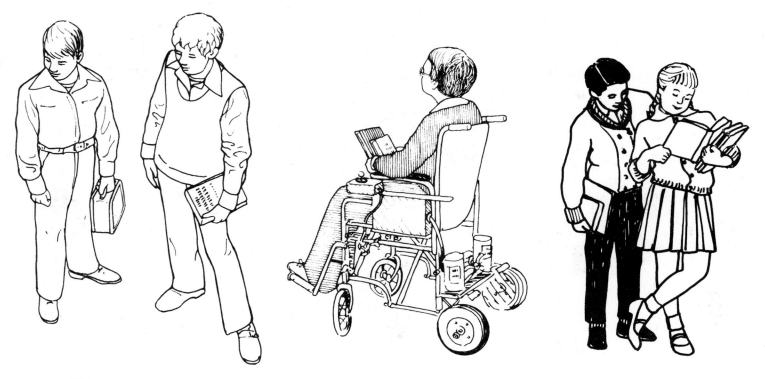

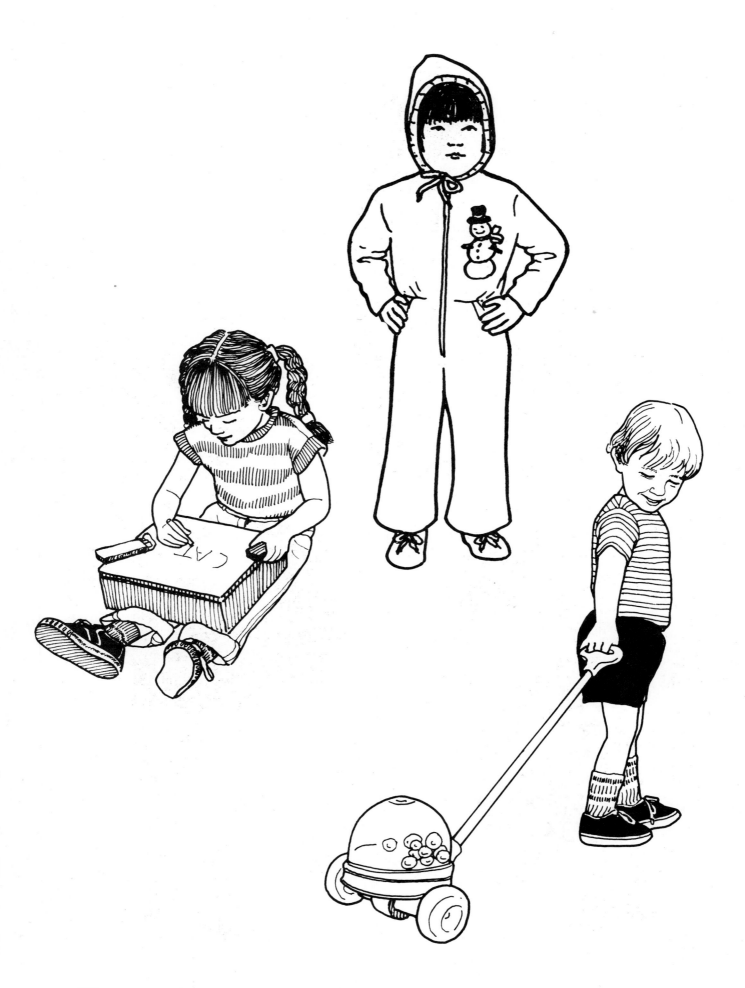

TREES

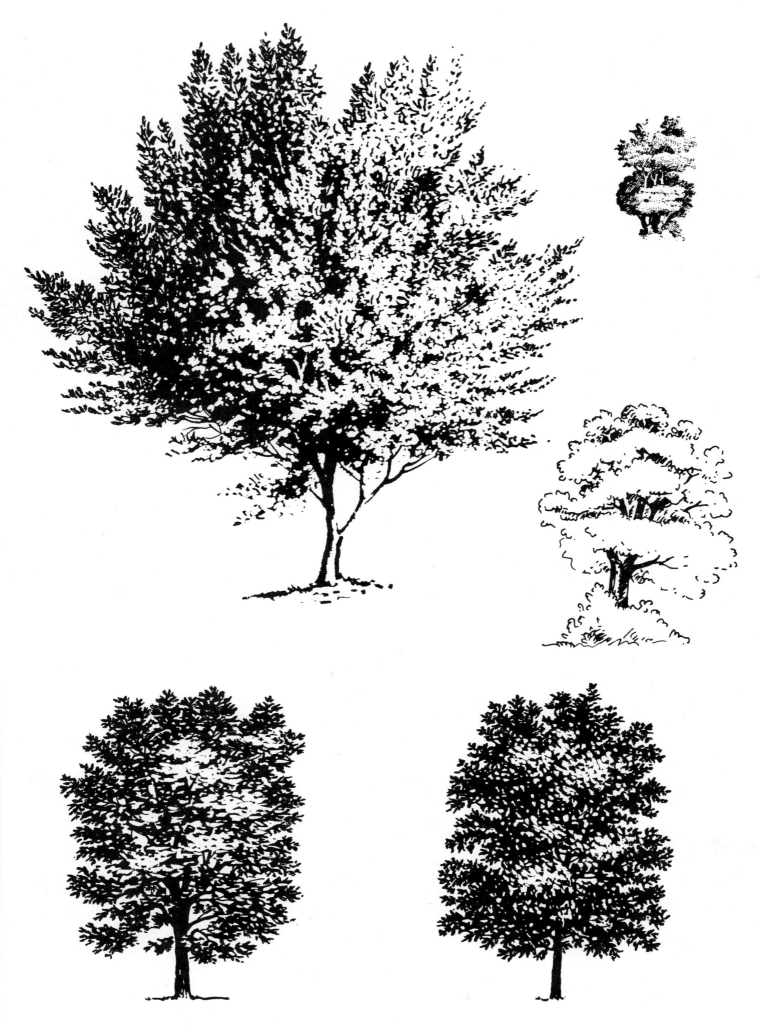

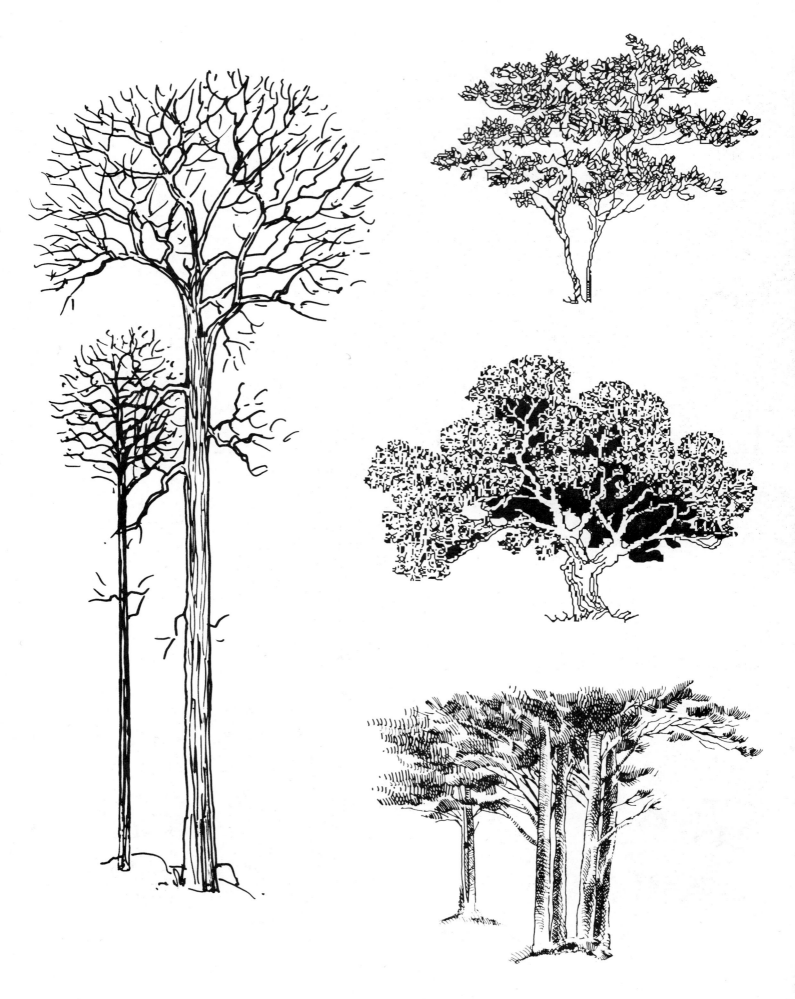

252

254

259

PLANTS

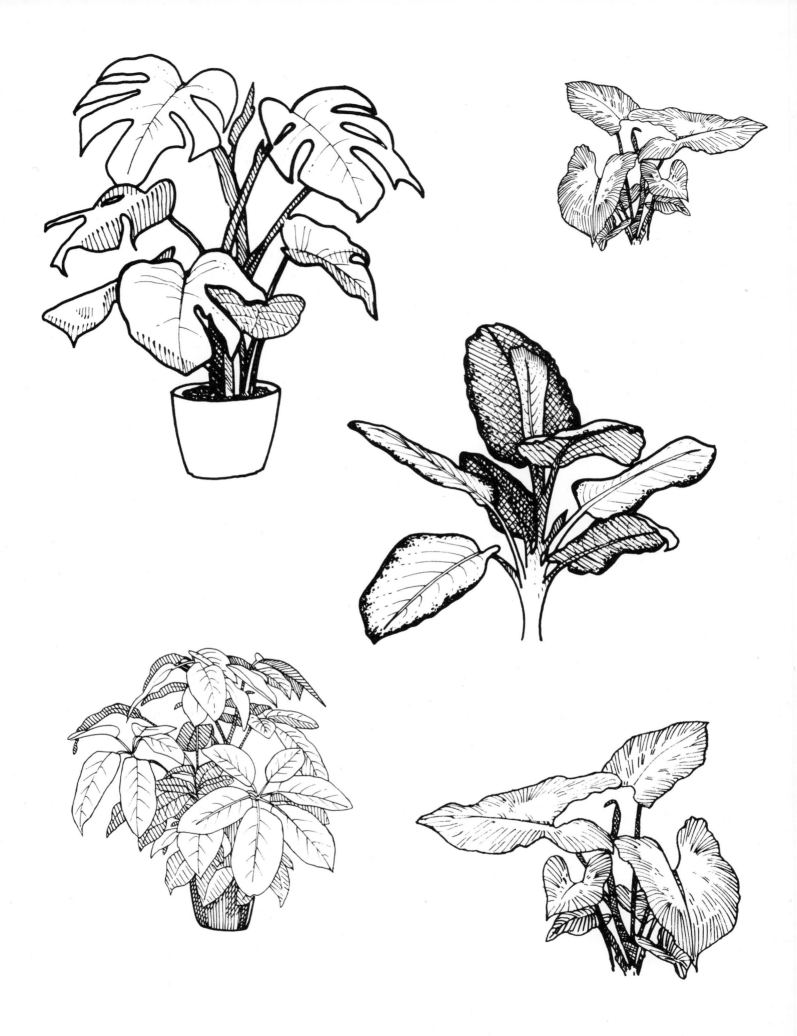

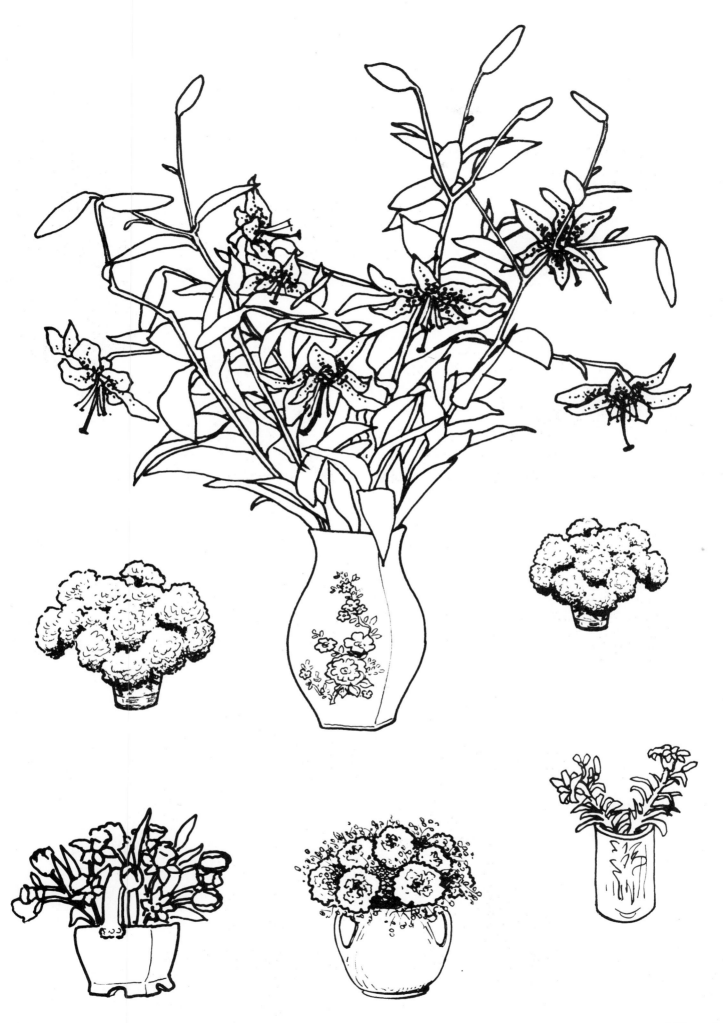

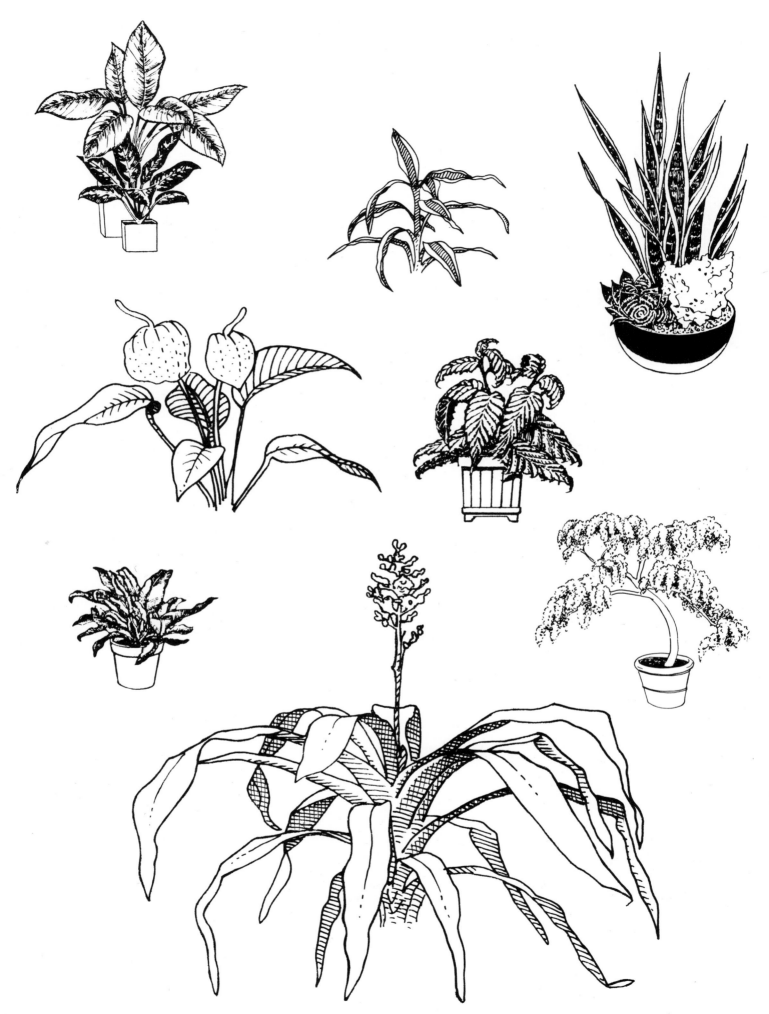

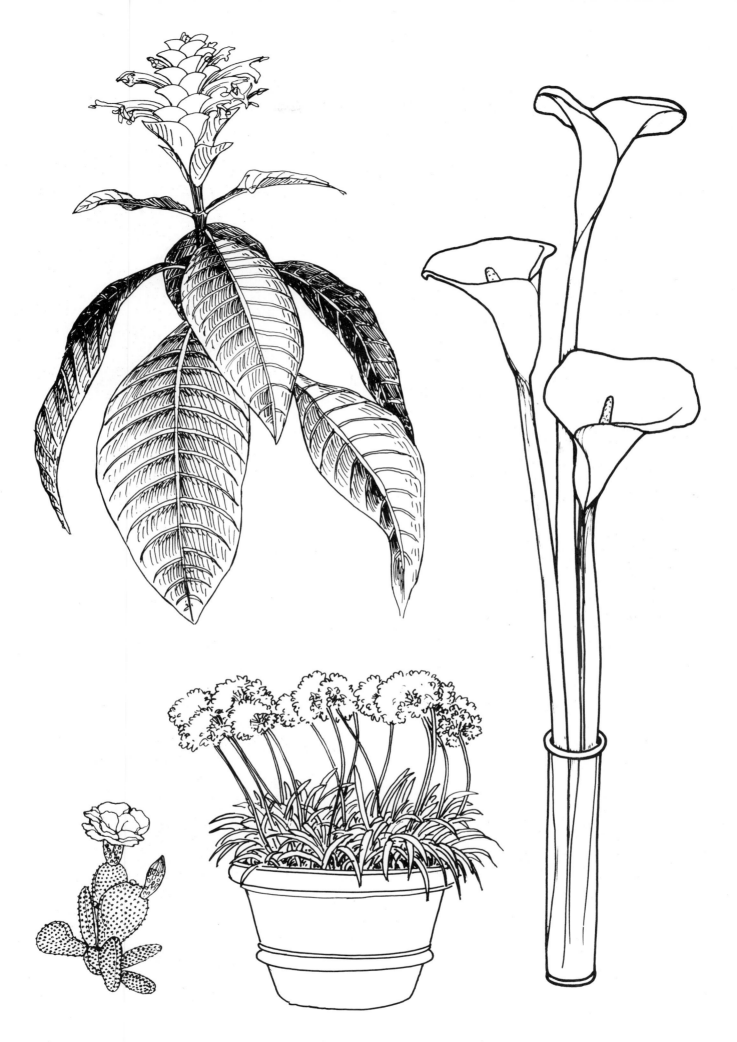

269

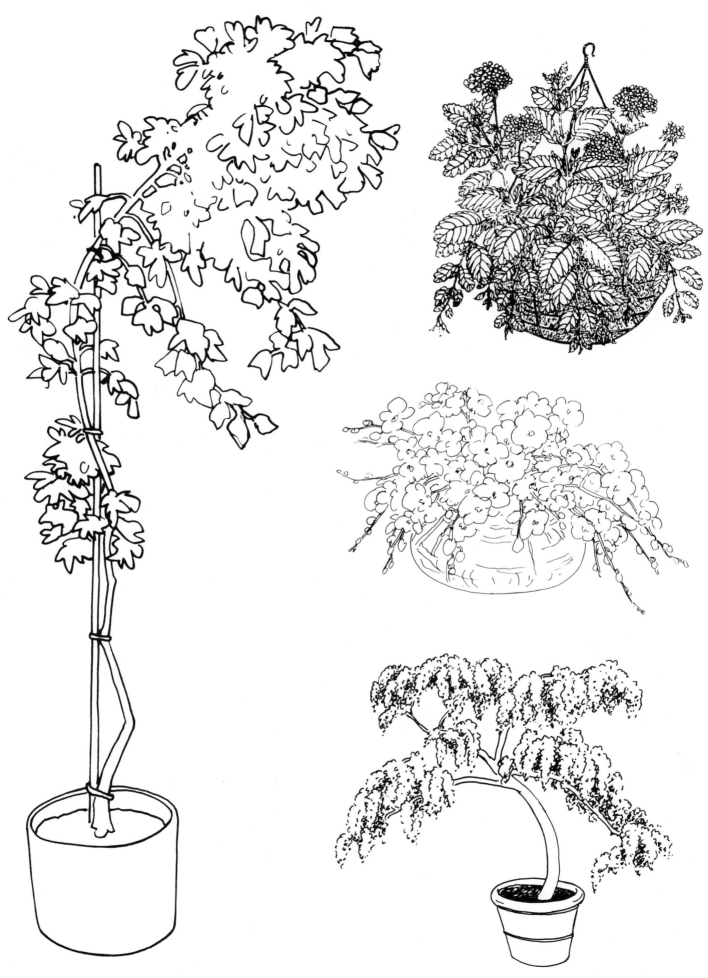

VEHICLES

SCALE 1/16"=1'

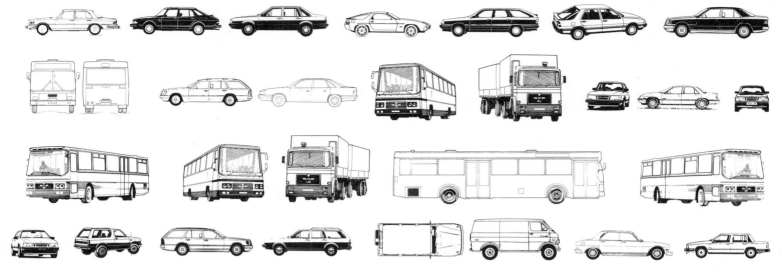

SCALE 1/8" = 1'

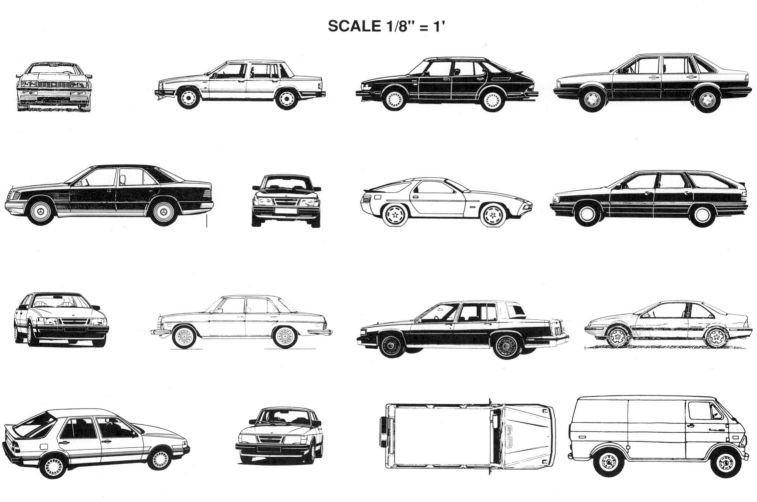

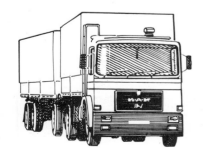

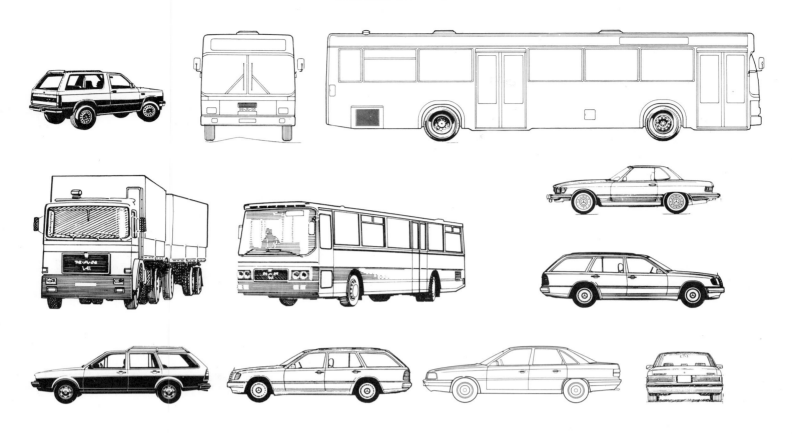

277

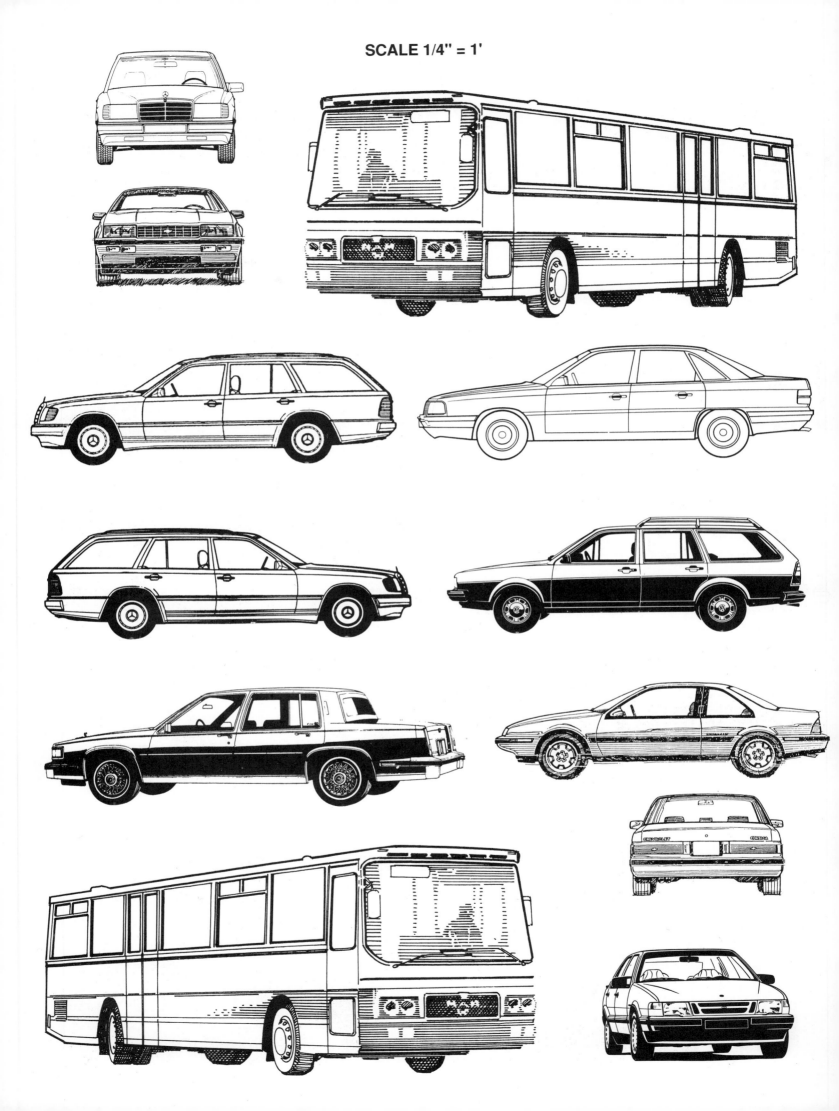

SCALE 1/4" = 1'

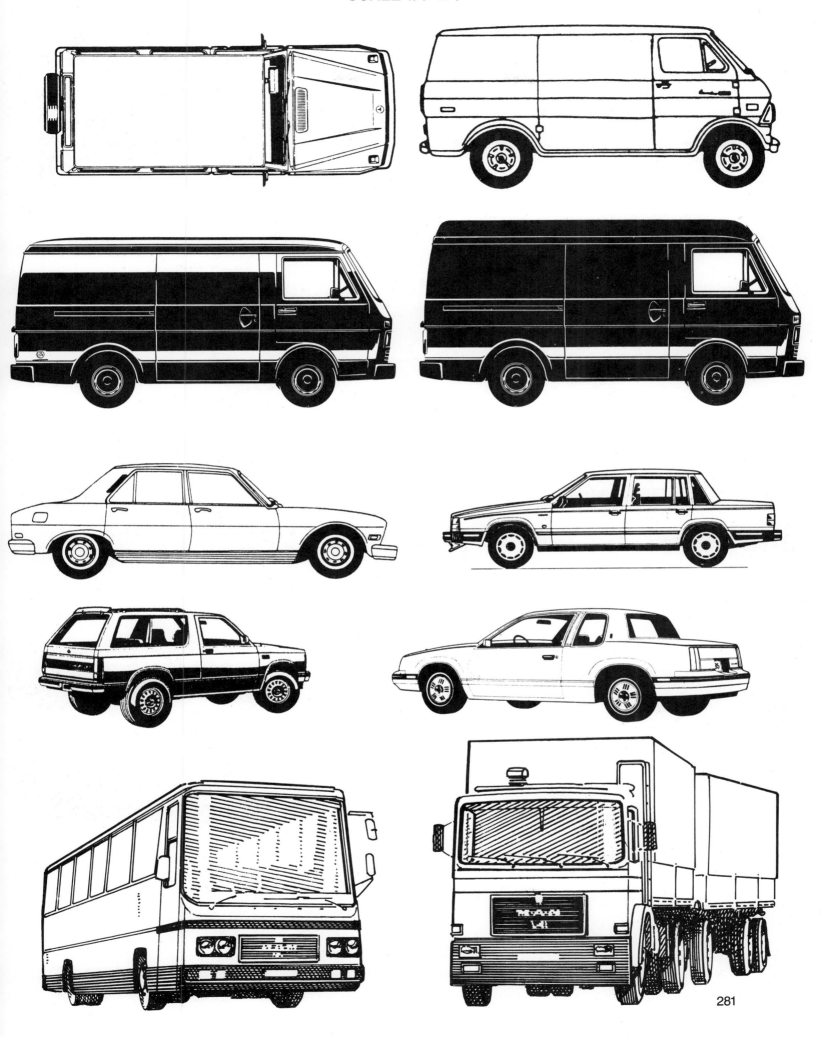

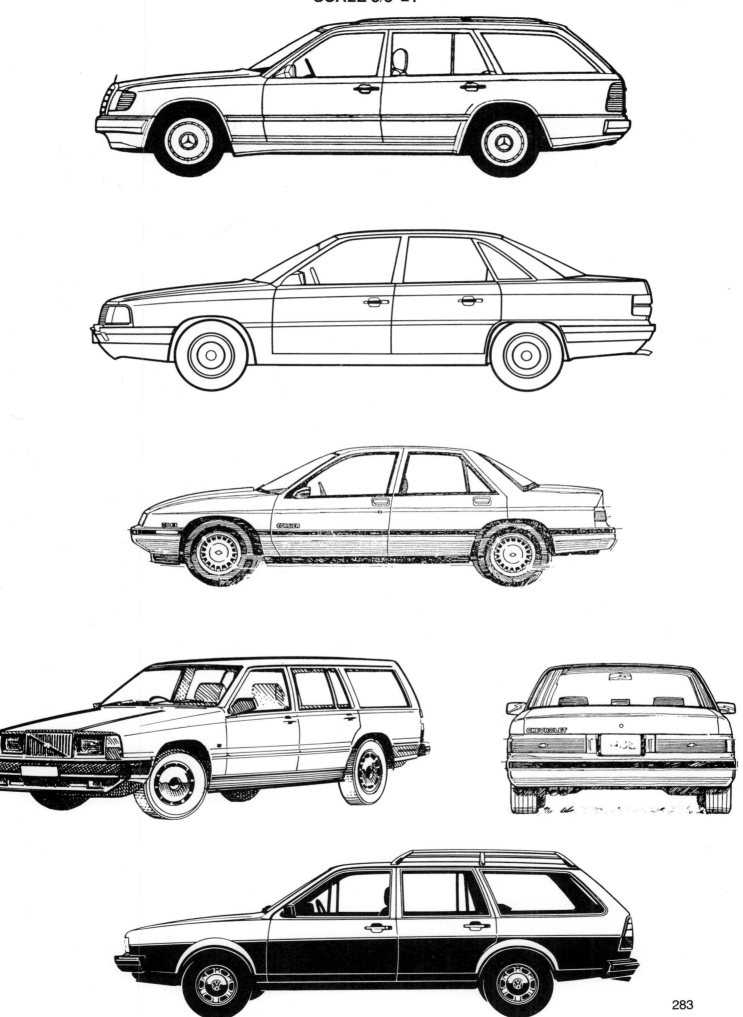

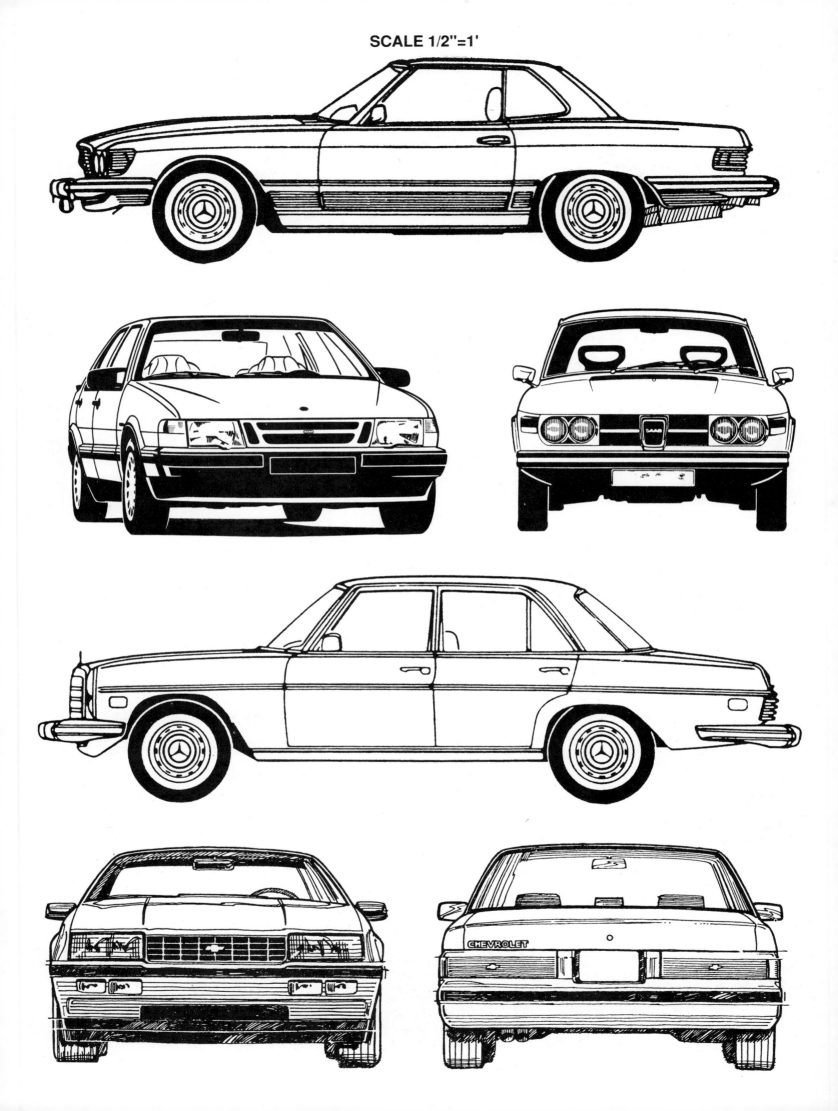

SCALE 1/2"=1'

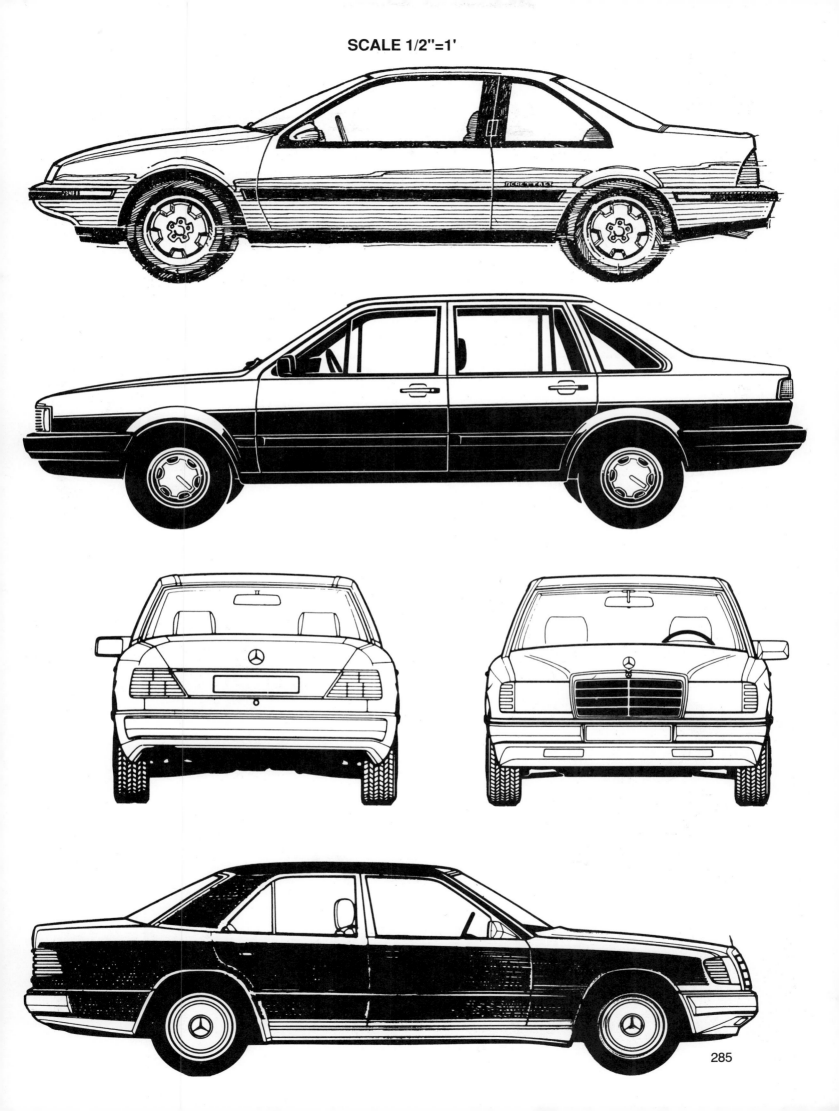

285

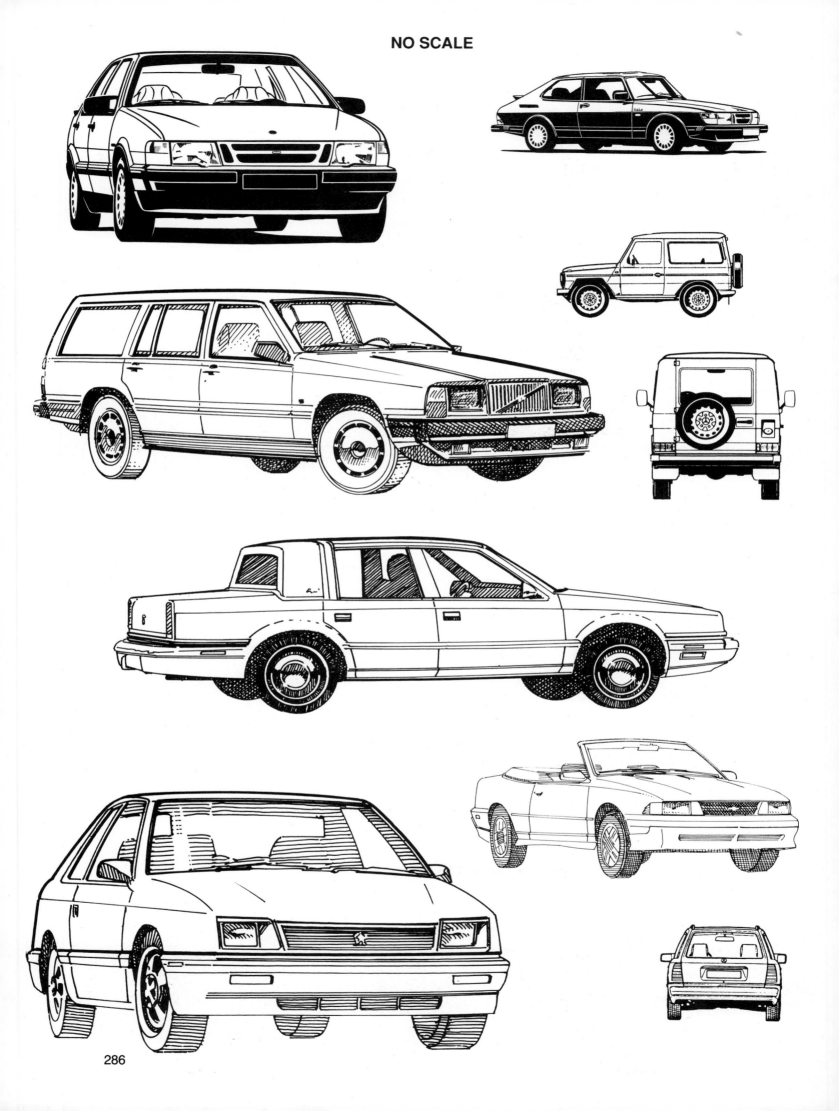

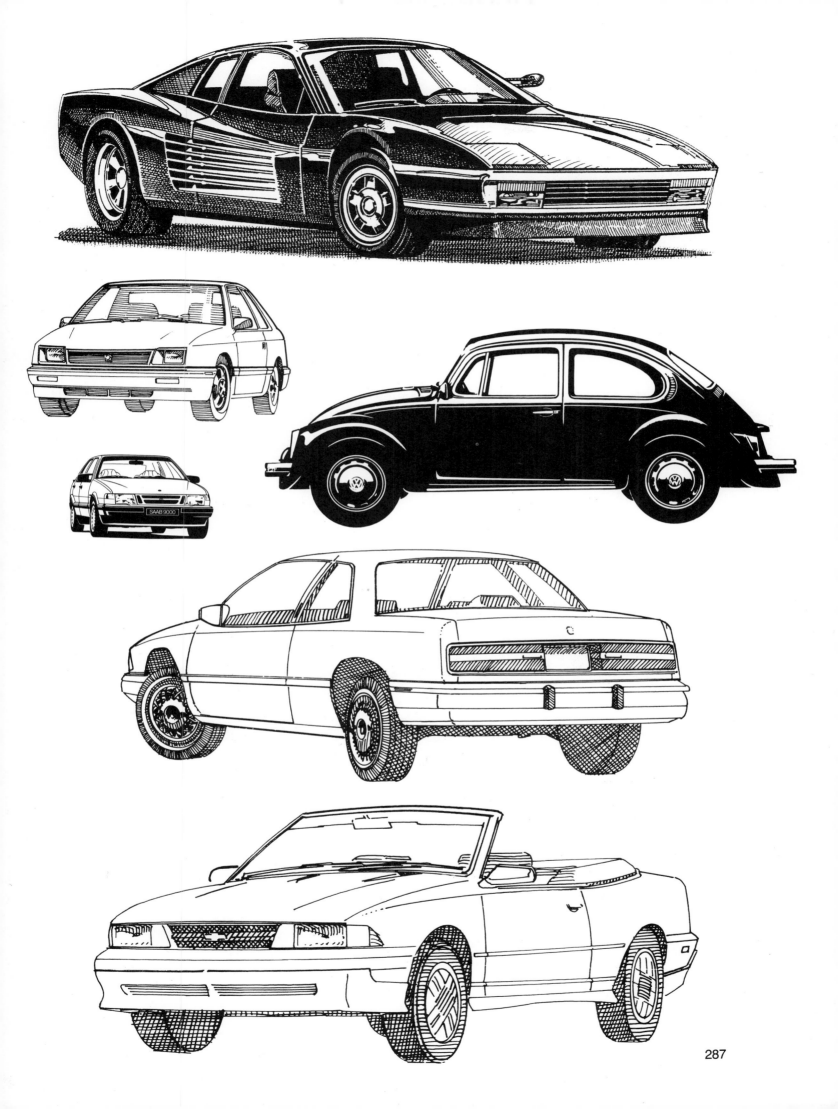